CHANGING AMERICA'S **ADJECTIVES** ONE CHILD AT A TIME

J. M. Rials

Tandem Light Press
950 Herrington Rd.
Suite C128
Lawrenceville, GA 30044

Copyright © 2021 by Janice Rials

All rights reserved. No part of this book may be reproduced, scanned, or transmitted in any printed, electronic, mechanical, including photocopying, recording, or any information storage and retrieval system, without permission in writing from the publisher. Please do not participate in or encourage piracy of copyrighted materials in violation of the author's rights.

Tandem Light Press paperback edition fall 2021

ISBN: 978-1-7376438-3-8

PRINTED IN THE UNITED STATES OF AMERICA

CONTENTS

Foreword v
Preface vii
Acknowledgments xi
Introduction: 1973. 1
Part I: Adults/Parent's Role. 7
Part II: Sharing Adjectives 13
Part III: Home Adjectives. 17
Part IV: Our Educational System's Role 21
Part V: Educators' Roles. 27
Part VI: The Media's Role. 31
Part VII: America's Adjectives. 33
Parent and Teacher Resources. 37
About the Author 63

FOREWORD

Changing America's Adjectives, One Child at A Time is Janice's second inspiring expression of love to children and families in the United States of America. Her first, *There Is No Moon at My House* is, similarly, an easy read, and wise advice to parents and teachers.

Changing America's Adjectives is a gentle guide to how we can make a paradigm shift. It is based on the construct that America is always changing, developing, and getting better. Written at a time of social and cultural turmoil, while a pandemic exposes the disparities that exist in this country, it captures how the words we speak affect how we treat or mistreat one another.

Janice's experiences in life, through the lens of a woman of color, a highly effective teacher, a wise and loving mother, grandmother, sister, and a devoted friend, give her a positive perspective on teaching us and our children. *Changing America's Adjectives* offers the opportunity and information we need to move forward through showing each other love and respect; teaching our children that social and cultural likenesses and differences make us strong; and speaking the adjectives that build us up as a nation.

– Dr. Sharron Jones

PREFACE

When I started writing this book it was during a time that three major events were taking place. There was a presidential election, it was the start of a shutdown caused by the Coronavirus, and the Black Lives Matter movement a march that was once again sparked by the killing of George Floyd and many other men and women of color. Because we were all in our homes and on social media, we watched as America showed a side of itself, I had thought we were working toward healing. Strangely enough, we had not.

The adjectives about America, which started to surface, were based on race, gender, religious belief, socioeconomic status, ability, inability, political party, fear, power, and the loss of power. When those nouns are accompanied by adjectives, their negative nature projects out into the world and causes more harm than healing. It is at this point that the message being sent to our children became a concern for me. The questions I asked were, "How do we change those negative adjectives?" and "Who plays what part in changing them?" The labels on America and its people at this time in history are not ones that I would want any child to ever use as a model for what they want to become.

Why one child at a time? Every human being on this Earth is born with what is called *agape love*, which is the highest level of unconditional love. Children's love is not based on your race, gender, religious belief, socioeconomic status, age, disability or ability, political party, or parental status. They love you no matter who you are. You have seen those cute little videos of toddlers running toward each other and giving the sincerest hug or kiss, young children playing together on playgrounds; they enter their educational journeys and come home so excited about the friends they have now decided will be their twins, sisters or brothers with no regard to race or any other negative adjectives adults use to determine how they treat each other. Children love regardless of their situations, as a student I had in my class once demonstrated during my earlier teaching years.

This was a child who had been labeled by the adults around them as having behavioral problems. They'd been labeled so many times that they had been placed in institutions that were supposed to help. During an episode in my classroom, as I was embracing them in order to prevent harm to themselves and others, I took the time to ask that child one important question. "Why are you acting up in school?" The reply is what shocked me! The child shared that their mom was in prison and they were going to keep acting up so they would get arrested and go to prison to be with their mom. None of the circumstances in which this child lived mattered; they loved their mother so much that they came up with a plan that they hoped would just bring them back together again, even if it was in prison. This is agape love.

Children carry and share this sense of agape until everyone who comes into contact or crosses paths with children, slowly affects the adjectives within them.

Oftentimes, we find ourselves putting labels on those we encounter throughout our lives, including our children, with little regard to the possible lifetime effect those adjectives and labels may have on our fellow man. It is my hope that by publishing this book, we all learn how to make sure our labels and their adjectives do not carry a lifetime of harm on ourselves as well as others. This change has to start at home, one child at a time.

ACKNOWLEDGMENTS

I want to thank God for trusting me with his visions, my daughter for your patience while working with me on yet another vision, Dr. Jones for your continued support, my family and friends that filled and continue to fill me with awesome adjectives, and, finally, Tandem Light Press for making another vision come to life.

INTRODUCTION
1973

IT WAS MY senior year in high school. I was so excited that after four years of high school it was finally my time to meet with my senior advisement counselor. As I entered his office, I was overjoyed with the fact that I had found the college that I wanted to attend. I entered his office with the college recruitment booklet, I had found in our school library, in my hand. As I sat down, I could hardly wait to share my choice of college I would attend after graduation. I proudly shared with Mr. __ that I wanted to attend the National College of Education in Evanston, IL. He let me go on and on about why I wanted to attend this college. It was now his turn to impart his senior advisement knowledge.

His first question was, "How did I find out about this school?" as if it were top-secret information.

I proudly showed him the booklet I had in my hand.

He went on to share what I thought was going to be how we were going to find the applications, and scholarship forms I would need to complete in order to attend the college of my choice. To my surprise, however, what he said was, "This is a private school and there are no Black students there." (That bit of knowledge I later found out was not true. There were indeed Black students at the National College of Education and they had just opened a campus in downtown Chicago.) He continued to share even more of his great advisement knowledge. Mr.__ went on to tell this excited student who had entered his office full of hopes and dreams of attending college, that it would be easier for her to get up from her chair, walk down to the nearest Cadillac dealership, and buy a new Cadillac than get into the National College of Education.

Oh, my goodness. The wonderful adjectives within me were now being taken over by some not-so-nice adjectives shared from an outside source—a school counselor. I was crushed for the rest of the day. By the time I made it home that day I was feeling like C-R-A-P!

My mom must have seen my face as I entered the kitchen. She broke out in song. "There she is, Miss America. There—she—is, Miss—America!" Now, my parents had always told us we could be and do anything if we worked hard, and to not try to beat our way by doing anything that takes advantage of others for personal gain, be it legal or illegal.

Just hearing her sing that song was all I needed. Just think, if my mom thought this little Black girl from the south side of Chicago could be Miss America in the 1970s, then, I could achieve anything.

I applied to the National College of Education, was accepted, and graduated with honors. I went on later in life to graduate with a bachelor's degree from Bradley University in Peoria, Illinois and received my master's from Piedmont University in Georgia. I hold with great pride the honor of being voted Local Teacher of The Year 2018–19.

That counselor's adjectives were powerful and had weight. The conversation we'd had was detrimental and could have changed the entire course of my life. Had I taken what he'd said and owned it, I may not have gone on to become a teacher and an author. This often happens when children do not have a strong support system at home or someone in their lives who believes in them. I share my story to say that as we journey through life, we are met with spoken as well as unspoken labels, which we carry with us regardless of race, age, gender, or socioeconomic status. It is the *adjectives* on those labels that can help or hinder a person.

ADJECTIVES

Webster's Dictionary defines adjectives as words that define or modify; that is, they limit or restrict the meaning of nouns.

If we were to rewrite this definition in regards to our children and adults, the definition would read as follows:

> **ADJECTIVES** are words that describe your child or other people in a way that either encourages or demolishes (destroys) their self-worth and abilities.

Do you remember the following old sayings: "I'm rubber, you are glue; whatever you say, bounces off of me and sticks to you!" Oh, how I wish this was true, but, in reality, those adjectives stick to us, and sometimes for a lifetime. Or "Sticks and stones may break my bones, but words will never hurt me." We often think that physical injury causes more pain and damage than words, but scientific research has found that positive and negative words not only affect us on a deep psychological level, but they have a significant impact on the outcome of our lives.

You start to acquire your adjectives as early as a newborn from the environment in which you were born. You then go on to gather even more from every adult you encounter, the media, social media, classmates, coaches, friends, family members, and even yourself. We all have what I call *inside adjectives*. They are the adjectives that stick like glue and you believe to be true about yourself. We also have *outside adjectives*. These are the adjectives said to you, which you let bounce off and not become how you define yourself.

We now understand that the labels are not the issue here. It is the adjectives we place on those labels, which are the problem. Let's take a look at how we all play a role in placing those adjectives on everyone's labels.

PART I
ADULTS/PARENT'S ROLE

> *"The manner in which we communicate and use language with our children can and most often will have a direct impact on how he views the world around him, as well as himself both in childhood and adulthood."*
>
> – KELI EWING, LPC

PARENTS PLAY A very crucial role in cultivating the adjectives within a family. Adjectives created within a family can become generational. Children pick up their adjectives through your conversations, your actions, and reactions, no matter their age. They are like sponges and absorb everything you say or do, as well as what you don't say or do.

Parents unconsciously apply adjectives they believe are helpful or encouraging but can be negatively comprehended by children. A mom would often use this phrase when her child helped her around the house, "You are such a **big** girl!" Only to find out that the child tied the compliment to her body image, causing her to overeat because she wanted to always be her mom's **big** girl. In fact, Mom had been speaking about the child's ability to help her.

Another way that parents unconsciously apply adjectives is through what I refer to as the give-and-take method. With all the things parents are faced with daily, we sometimes get overwhelmed and react before we think. How many times have you done this before?

Your child comes running down the hall all excited because they have finally achieved a goal or completed a project that they had been trying to achieve for quite some time. It could be as simple as drawing a picture to get a passing grade in school. Your reply: "Great job! But look at your floor. It is a mess!"

The positive adjective "Great!" sent the message of "You are great and can do anything if you keep working at it." That was then taken away and replaced with "No matter what I do, I am not good enough."

Unconsciously applied negative adjectives can have the same effect as verbal abuse on a child. It's universally accepted in the research, that for every negative adjective a child encounters, it takes five or more positive adjectives to counteract its effect, and even more once that child has made it an inside adjective.

Think back on your interactions with your children today and ask yourself: have your positive adjectives outnumbered your negative adjectives today?

EASY ADJECTIVES

Often, we find it easier to express positive adjectives that connect to children's outward physical appearances rather than their intellect and or character.

"You are so pretty!"

"Look how cute you are in that outfit!"

"You are so handsome."

"Look at your beautiful hair."

The overuse of outward-appearance adjectives can destroy children's intellectual confidence and character. Children grow up thinking that their self-worth as well as that of others, is based solely on the clothes they wear or how they look. As a result, children oftentimes are quick to use the adjectives poor, ugly, not pretty, or nerd on others. They will use non-verbal cues, like only wanting to play with other children who look like or dress as they do. They use outward appearances to choose their friends. Adjectives like princess, king, beautiful, baby, when overly used give a sense of entitlement, which may cause them to believe that they are inherently deserving of privileges or special treatment. As parents, you must celebrate your child's intellect and character. Children need to hear their parents using positive adjectives that relate to their character and intellect as well as that of others:

"You are such a **smart** young lady."

"Mommy made a **wonderful** dinner tonight."

"You have a very **creative** mind."

"**Awesome** job, Buddy."

"That was very **kind** of you to help your friend."

"Wow! Daddy, you did a **great** job combing Mika's hair."

Children, hearing these types of adjectives, grow up able to give as well as receive positive adjectives. They become their inner voices when faced with negative outside adjectives.

Thank you, Mom, for my Miss America song!

FATHERS

Dads often get the short end of the stick when it comes to their roles within our families. Yes, we look to Dad to be the protector and provider but, regardless if they are in the home or not, they too have an important role of adjective changer.

You are the person who determines what future adjectives will be used to define families for generations to come. You give your daughters the adjectives needed to build the qualities their future husbands should have. You are the one who will produce the adjectives of what being a husband and father should be. You provide the adjectives your sons will use to describe or address the women in their lives. You define the adjectives your sons and daughters will or will not find acceptable when they go out into the world. Your adjectives will either encourage or discourage. Most importantly, you, and only you, form the adjectives that will either make you proud or destroy your legacy. Dads, take a moment and look at your legacy as it is today. Are your adjectives ones that will cultivate positive adjectives for generations to come? Will they make you proud or destroy your legacy?

MOTHERS

As a mom, you are a very significant adjective provider and changer. The adjectives you use when speaking with your children will be the adjectives they will use when speaking to their children and to others. Your adjectives will provide the adjectives your sons will hope their future wives will possess. The adjectives you use when talking to and about your children's dad will be the adjectives your daughters will use when talking to and about the father of their children. Your adjectives will instill confidence or doubt, love or hate, kindness or cruelty, compassion or indifference. Your adjectives will either build up or break down generations to come.

Moms, take a moment to ponder this. What will

your families look like, in generations to come, based on the adjectives you have used within your household?

> *"While perfection as a parent is an unattainable goal, the words and the tone parents use can tremendously influence a child's sense of self."*
> — Steven Oshin, M.A.L.

PART II
SHARING ADJECTIVES

AS PARENTS, WE also share our own adjectives with our children. Schoolwork and behavior issues seem to attract the adjectives that are shared most often. This most often occurs in the areas that a child may be struggling in.

"I was a **horrible** math student!"

"I was **bad** in school."

Not only do parents tell their child's teacher this, but parents also love sharing these adjectives with their children whenever they struggle with various subjects or behavioral issues themselves. Children now take their parent's negative adjectives and make them their own. They often label themselves with adjectives: not good enough, a loser, dummy, not smart, annoying, bad, mean, etc. We now have two generations with excuses to not even try to do well in school or any other area that will require them to work just a little harder to achieve success. To turn this around, children need to hear adjectives that support them to become successful.

"Remember the way we studied your addition facts and you did an outstanding job on your test? We can do this again."

When parents use adjectives that foster encouragement, confidence, and pride in situations where children face what they deem to be a failure or not—according to their parent's expectations—all is not lost and the negative adjectives will be replaced with: I can do anything, I am good enough, I am not a loser or dummy, and I am just as smart as anyone else.

The most damaging adjectives parents like to share with their children are the ones that occur when the parents are in turmoil, divorce, or single parenting. As a parent, you are the ones who chose each other. It is not the child's fault if it does not work out. The worst thing you could ever engage a child in is the sharing of those negative adjectives you are feeling. I spoke earlier about children's unconditional love for their parents; well, it is no different for your children. Now, you may feel that the other parent is the worst person in the world, but that is your opinion. It is not your job to convince your child to feel the same way. You must be careful when speaking to or about their parent. You may not be talking directly to your child but those adjectives that are within earshot can distress and make an impression because they are still exposed and listening to your conversations. As a single mom myself, I know how you feel when your child is sitting and waiting on the other parent to arrive and they don't show up. There is nothing more heartbreaking to you as a parent than to watch your child sitting and looking out the window at every passing car or jumping up when the phone or doorbell rings in hope that they will come for an outing or a phone call they have promised your child. No matter how upset this makes you, please, do not share your negative adjectives with your child about their parent. I have experienced this with my child but at no time have I ever spoken ill of my child's dad. My obligation was to be the soft place to land after disappointment. My reply to "Mommy, what happened?" or "Why didn't he come?" was a simple truth, "I don't know." I would then find something fun for her to do if her dad was a no-show.

The adjectives and opinions of my daughter's father were totally hers. She formed them based on the relationship she has experienced with her dad. The funny thing is, when she got married, she had her dad walk her halfway down the aisle, and my dad—her grandfather—the rest of the way, giving honor to them both.

Remember the agape love I spoke of at the beginning of this book. Even though her dad missed play dates and other things in her life, she still loves him unconditionally. As a parent, you must allow your child to form his or her own opinion, labels, and adjectives of their parents based on their experiences. You must allow them to have this experience with the other parent so long as no harm will come to them in doing so. If the adjectives formed during this time are not ones they have formed on their own, it can destroy the relationship between you and your child when and if they find out otherwise.

PART III
HOME ADJECTIVES

CHILDREN REALLY DO listen to you. They take in your every word. Have you ever listened to your children as they play on your phone? The first time you hear this you stand in astonishment at how they sound just like you. Because of this, you must be aware of the adjectives you or others are using directly or indirectly around your children.

The adjectives used within a home are just as important as those outside your home. Adjectives used inside your home do not just stay within your home. There are members of your family that love sharing your adjectives with others. A large number of our adjectives come from within our homes. As adults, sometimes our daily life struggles can get the better of us; but, as adults, we must be very diligent in the word choices we use around and to children, no matter their ages. Some of the worst adjectives and phrases are used during adult interactions with their own and other's children around them. There have been times in which we all have been in parks, malls, restaurants, schools, or as guests in other homes where adults use the following adjectives when talking to or about children (the following adjectives may be a little harsh but it is the truth that provokes change): **idiot, dumbass, loser, freak, stupid, ugly, badass, fat, evil, trash, bitch, a mistake, did not want you anyway,** you are such **a dummy,** you are **lazy** just like your___, you are a **loudmouth** just like your___, etc. These are only a few of the adjectives shared by children during the research before writing this book.

As parents and adults, it is our obligation to guard our children against such negative adjectives. My daughter was about two years old when we were invited to a household that I had never been to previously but we knew they had small children. We ended up not staying because the parents of the children who lived there addressed their children in ways I had never been around. I thought to myself who calls their children by saying, "Bring your badass here!" That was all I needed to hear and, at that point, we left and never went back to their home. It was not important to me if they remained friends or not. As parents, we have a responsibility to not expose our children to such negative adjectives. It really did not matter that they did not become our friends. Our child's wellbeing is and was always more important than any friendship.

As a parent, not only should this be unacceptable outside your home, it should not be acceptable within your home. As children growing up, we could not call our siblings or friends anything other than their names or nicknames and the word stupid or dumb was totally unacceptable. Some adjectives were not allowed while playing or at any other time, nor do I recall my parents using curse words when they were talking to us or anyone else.

As a parent, when you find that situation has pushed or will push you to use negative adjectives as your form of communication, *Stop, take a deep breath, and remove yourself* for a little while. Come back later and speak with your child because once that negative adjective is used, you cannot take it back and the damage is done. Negative adjectives can ruin a parent-child relationship because over time you come to see that child as just that adjective.

Always keep in mind that a child raised with negative adjectives, will become those negative adjectives and share them with others; but a child raised with positive adjectives, will become those positive adjectives and share them with others. Make sure the adjectives you use are the ones that will provide encouragement and support for generations to come.

PART IV
OUR EDUCATIONAL SYSTEM'S ROLE

PARENTS, EVEN THOUGH this section title is Our Educational System's Role, this chapter will aid you with what to look for when you bring your children to school. Also, when you find a gap, you can do your part to help your child and the teacher be successful. Our educational system plays a very significant role in aiding our children with adjectives once they enter our educational system; be it public or private. The most telling part of how our educational system fosters adjectives is through the curriculum taught in the school systems across the United States of America.

I had the opportunity to be at my grandchild's house during her online lesson on American History as I was writing this book. She is in her third year of high school and this is her first encounter with American history. I asked my older grandchildren if this was true for them also and surprisingly, they'd had the same experiences. The first very brief assignment was on slavery in the United States of America. It contained language that spoke so wonderfully of how enslaved people were accompanied to America by various ship owners. When I read the term accompanied, I thought of two or more people going to a place by choice. For example, you would accompany your wife on a night out on the town or your children to a special event. The sad part about this is that I had the same lessons. I saw the same pictures of the enslaved people laid out neatly in single rows, or on plantations smiling, dancing, and just having a wonderful time. My classmates, both Black and white, saw this too, and, because of this, some 156 years later, I know of people that make statements such as, "I don't understand why African Americans are so upset about slavery. Enslaved people had food, clothing, and shelter."

Now, I don't fault them so much because of the Daughters of the Confederacy's hand in writing America's history books after the Civil War. We teach that Christopher Columbus and other European Explorers were the founders of this country. If we tell our truth about the beginning of the United States of America, that it was not found or discovered but was taken from the Native Americans then we see that there are only three ways in which every one of America's original families came to be in America:

1. They were born of this land: Native Americans
2. They were brought here by force: Slavery
3. They chose to come: Immigrants from other countries.

Just as with the lessons of slavery, Native Americans are depicted negatively and out of sequence in our students' history lessons and books.

Teachers in K-12 are still teaching lessons with the same negative aspects set forth by the Daughters of the Confederacy after the Civil War. You know the saying: "He who holds the pen writes the history!" It is time to give the pen to those who will write the truth.

Telling our truth would be a magnificent start to healing our country by teaching our children from Pre-K-12th grade. Although our history is one of cruelty and mistreatment, it is also one of awesome adjectives that would foster encouragement, determination, and perseverance.

Just think of how proud every child would be if everyone could read their people's stories and the obstacles they faced along with their outstanding achievements. I am sixty-five years old, and I often think about how great and proud I would have felt if my classmates and I had read about the African Americans that went from slavery to building their own flourishing towns, doctors, lawyers, and inventors; learning about the great inventors of products we still use today instead of those lessons that produced *distorted, negative, and laughable* adjectives, which are still expressed today in our classrooms.

Oh, how proud I would have been as we sat in class reading through our schoolbooks in kindergarten to twelfth grade. We would have learned how we all help build this country and that every one of us had the potential to develop communities that could support themselves just like they did in Tulsa, Oklahoma 1906–1921: Black Wall Street. These are positive adjectives!

Throughout our school years, we would have all learned that sports, music, and entertainment are not the only careers we could strive to succeed in. We would have read how, as far back as the seventeenth and eighteenth century, just about everything we use today was an invention of an African American and that it is okay to dream! Just this morning, I bet you used some of those items.

You woke up in a comfortable bed that was not on the floor because it is on a **bed frame/bedstead**; you walked into the bathroom to a **toilet/water closet**; you reached for the **doorknob,** which you used to open doors all day; while in your office, your pencil broke. You had to use the **pencil sharpener** sitting on your desk. Suppose you needed to take a break to clear your head after working so hard. You could go outside and ride around on your bicycle because it has a **bicycle frame**. When your day was complete, you felt safe in your home because you remembered to set your **home security system**. By the way, I taught this lesson, which prompted a parent to go to the district office and report that I was distorting American history. She then withdrew her student from my class and the school. See, she would have had a different mindset had she been in our classroom. Our classmates would have seen that they also could have gone on to be awesome…

Mathematicians and scientists: We all would have learned that there are unlimited opportunities beyond our surroundings, just like NASA's three hidden figures, whose accomplishments for years were hidden and never told. Girls of all races would have discovered that *girls can do math* and send people to the moon! We would have had classmates who might have been inspired to go on to become outstanding…

American pioneers in science: Like the first African American doctors in the US: James McCune Smith and Rebecca Crumpler, or Daniel Hale Williams who not only became the first doctor to perform open-heart surgery in the US, but also opened Provident Hospital in Chicago in 1891. One of us could hold the cure for cancer or Covid-19 in our hands.

Finally, we all would have learned that our government should be just as diverse as the people it is elected to serve. They are also the people's voice in our country because we all have the potential to go on to be upstanding…

Politicians: We would have learned that if we are not pleased with what is happening to our classmates or communities, we could grow up and have careers in politics and make a positive difference because our forefathers have already achieved it. As early as the 1800s, native Americans, African Americans, and white Americans all held political office at some time for the good of all Americans.

Our educational system and fellow Americans tell of other countries' stories and the suffrage they endured and survived—the Holocaust, French Revolution, the Cambodian genocide, apartheid, etc—but we refuse to speak our truth. This has led us to where we are now. Parents, and our educational system, can change our children's adjectives by telling our whole truth during our children's educational journeys. As parents, we cannot just place the responsibility solely on the school system; we must work hand in hand—do the research, visit museums, and watch documentaries with your children, so they may grow up respecting and honoring everyone's truths.

PART V
EDUCATORS' ROLES

CLASSROOM TEACHERS ARE often restricted about what they are allowed to teach outside of the curriculum provided by the school district. They still play a very important role in changing children's adjectives though. There are some awesome adjectives being fostered within classrooms but we must address the negative ones that are within the classrooms, too. Students have been labeled with the following negative adjectives by their fellow classmates—remember reading earlier about children gladly sharing the adjectives they bring from home with others? School is where they often share them.

Students have been labeled with adjectives such *as stupid, dumb, annoying, weird, bully, sad, nerd, ugly, mean, crazy, lazy, not good enough, loser, trash, fat,* and even *racist* by other students. They may have also been made to feel this way by their teacher's actions within their classrooms, according to a student survey conducted for this book. As educators, we must be very conscious of the adjectives fostered within our classrooms. Negative adjectives can be unconsciously brought about when teachers only call on the students they know have the correct answers or the kid who raises their hand for every question. This may cause someone in the class to feel the negative adjectives associated with not being smart enough or good enough.

As the teacher in the class, come up with ways that do not require students to raise their hands. Students can be given thinking time and names drawn from a container of ping pong balls, craft sticks with their names on them, or maybe assigned numbers.

As the leader in a classroom, when you have a student who you have deemed to have a behavioral problem, be aware that students will accuse that same child of any issues that occur within your classroom; students form negative adjectives about these children because of their prior behaviors. As the classroom teacher, what you don't say is just as important as what you do say.

Negative adjectives should not be allowed from anyone on school grounds. If you don't address it when it occurs, you give students permission to pile the negative adjectives onto their classmates. You must be aware of your body language and facial expressions when students respond in ways you did not expect.

As a classroom teacher, you have the potential to be a great catalyst for promoting positive adjectives in students' lives. First, you must identify and own your own unconscious biases and assumptions, and, yes, we all have them. Some assumptions made by teachers are: It is always boys that are out of control in classes; girls are not good in certain subjects such as math and science. As an educator, you must be aware of being more forgiving of students' behaviors because they are on school teams, their grades, or affiliations. Next, you must understand that every child's household does not look like yours or anyone else's in your class. You must respect your students' experiences because those are their experiences and realities. You should not make assumptions based on your experiences. An example of this would be, making statements such as "Why is that well-dressed student receiving free lunch?" Or "If that child's parent can afford to buy those gym shoes, why don't they take her to the dentist?"

As I sat here writing this section of the book, it caused me to think about how my own labels and adjectives in school might have been different. I was raised in a household that did not agree with us answering with "Yes, sir" and "No, ma'am." Had I been raised in the south, some teachers might have labeled me with the adjective of being disrespectful. In fact, it was a cultural choice my parents made because they had to address white America that way, no matter how they treated them while growing up in the south.

As an educator who cultivates positive adjectives within your classroom, you must have some knowledge of the students and their cultures, which enter your class, and not just the adjectives that are passed down year after year from fellow teachers. Talk to your parents and get to know them; they love sharing.

Finally, remember each year, as you prepare your classroom to welcome your students, look around and see if every child is represented on your bookshelves, posters, and bulletin boards. As Rudine Sims Bishop writes in *Mirrors, Windows, and Sliding Glass Doors*, "When children cannot find themselves reflected in the books they read, or when the images they see are distorted, negative, or laughable, they learn a powerful lesson about how they are devalued in the society of which they are a part."

Ask yourself, throughout the school year, have you read a book, taught a lesson, showed a video, made a project, or at least sang a song, that would make every child feel valued and proud to be who they are. When your students entered your classroom, they were somebody; and when they leave your classroom at the end of the year, they should be a better somebody filled with wonderful adjectives.

Thank you, Mrs. Clarkfeather (Altgeld Elementary), Mrs. Kennedy–Bond (Upper Grade Center), Mrs. Burns Harper (HS), and Mr. Shelton–Harper (HS) for all of your positive adjectives, which I still carry today.

PART VI
THE MEDIA'S ROLE

IT IS OFTEN said that the media will be the downfall of mankind. If you take a really good look at that statement, you will see that it is completely false. The media is not the cause of the negative labels and adjectives that appear on it. There has never been a television that produces one show, or a commercial that depicts people in negative ways, or shows of American families of only one ethnicity as if other families don't exist. Not one cell phone has ever produced tweets, Facebook posts, Instagram messages, etc., that caused people to commit suicide, harm themselves, or just feel unloved. Not one newspaper, magazine, or book has ever written or displayed pictures of false or misleading information on its own. There has never been a song that has written itself, which degrades women, glamorizes illegal activity, and sends the message that it is okay to use language such as bitch, hoe, n*g**r when referring to other human beings. Never has there been a movie that has created, filmed, produced, or sponsored itself that negatively depicts other cultures or excludes production of positive movies that just might change a few adjectives. Not one video game has ever made the games that are played on them.

The adjectives from the various forms of media are derived from the humans who compose the content and then send it out via those various forms of media, which then bleed negative adjectives onto our children.

It is clear, therefore, that the media will not cause our downfall and that we are in control of it all. You can make the choice to help change America's adjectives, one child at a time, through that device you control.

PART VII
AMERICA'S ADJECTIVES

LAST BUT NOT least, America has adjectives that will affect children throughout their lives.

Imagine living in a home where your mom and dad used their power and positions to gain personal wealth with no regard to how it would affect their children.

Imagine those same parents had been chosen to represent you and have your best interests at heart but instead do everything within their power to keep their children oppressed and separated.

Imagine living in a home where you and your siblings are judged by the color of your skin, the texture of your hair, your gender, your economic status, which they control, or merely the bedroom in which you reside.

Imagine living in a home where truth does not

matter and neither parent is willing to stand up for what is right and true.

Imagine living in a home where rules and systems are put in place, which will not allow you and your siblings to grow up and provide for yourselves or future generations because the jobs and resources needed, have been given to your neighbors, in order to ensure that you and your siblings will continue to struggle.

Imagine living in a home where you make more money doing nothing than you do if you went to work every day and your parents won't do a simple thing such as raising the minimum wage to help make it possible to feed, clothe, and provide shelter for yourself.

Just imagine a home where your parents fear their children's truth, strength, and ability so much that they put in place rules and regulations that will cause you and your siblings to be placed in a new version of oppression: prison, unemployment, alcoholism, and drug abuse.

Imagine a home where you were given the right to vote by your grandparents, but your parents removed the voting boxes, closed the polling stations near you, and made you bring your vote to them personally no matter your ability, and made it a crime to give out water or food to those standing in long lines to cast a vote. Then, when they count your vote, they accuse you of cheating.

Imagine living in a home where you and your siblings are told of only one side of your family's history and the other side's is left out as if their lives did not matter to them, and even the history told to you was whitewashed so that it sounds better than it really was.

Imagine living in a home where your sisters and brothers are treated differently when they walk out the door, only to have some not return at all, based on the color of their skin.

Imagine living in a home where someone is allowed to purchase weapons and then discharge them into your home or school because your parents do not want to upset an organization that happens to be funding them.

The home I speak of is ours, the United States of America. The parents I speak of are the adults; no matter their position, whether they are elected or not. The largest contributors of the adjectives come from among us. We are a country that has brought about some of the greatest as well as the worst adjectives imaginable, and until we come to understand and recognize that every American matters, the adjectives we produce will affect all of our children and generations to come, at some point in their lives. As Americans, we all play a role in which adjectives are formed about us. We must all understand that no matter your age, race, gender, or position in life, every drug you sell, make, or buy; every carjacking; every robbery; every life that you take; each vote you don't cast; every elected official you put into positions that do not portray the types of adjectives you would like your children to take possession of; every day that you don't attend school; every child that you bring into this world and then not be the parent they need you to be; every time you foster hate and fear of those who have beliefs, thoughts or looks that are different than yours; every time you see or hear of an injustice and stay silent, you too are helping form those negative adjectives your children and generations to come will have to fight against.

Faber and Mazlish said it best in this quote taken from *Liberated Parents, Liberated Children*, "It might help if we think of a child's self-image as wet cement. Imagine that each of our responses to him leaves a mark and shapes his character. Over time the cement hardens with our message firmly embedded."

With what adjectives will children leave after crossing your path?

Every label has an adjective on it that may be difficult to remove but it is never too late to change it. Let's change our adjectives, America, one child at a time so, we can all stand tall and say we are proud to be Americans!

> *"We are the ones we've been waiting for. We are the change that we seek!"*
>
> – BARACK OBAMA

PARENT AND TEACHER RESOURCES

*Children's Books to Read Aloud and
Share with your Children:*

Awesome Adjective Changers
by Janice Rials

We All Sing with The Same Voice
by J. Philip Miller and Sheppard M. Greene

A Sick Day for Amos McGee
by Philip C. Stead

Each Kindness
by Jacqueline Woodson

Last Stop on Market Street
by Matt De La Pena

Those Shoes
by Maribeth Boelts

Ordinary Mary's Extraordinary Deed
by Emily Pearson and Fumi Kosaka

The Invisible Boy
by Trudy Ludwig

Enemy Pie
by Derek Munson

Words And Your Heart
by Kate Jane Neal

Hooray For Hat
by Brian Won

Thank You, Omu
by Oge Mora

A Hat For Mrs. Goldman
by Michelle Edwards

I Walk With Vanessa
by Kerascoet

The Cool Bean
by Jory John and Pete Oswald

The Color Collector
by Nicholas Solis

Adrian Simcox Does Not Have a Horse
by Marcy Campbell

What Is Given From The Heart
by Patricia C. McKissack

The Power Of One
by Trudy Ludwig

We're All Wonders
by R.J. Palacio

We're Different, We're the Same
by Bobbi Kates

Just Ask!
by Sonia Sotomayor

A Hundred Thousand Welcomes
by Mary Lee Donovan

I Am Enough
by Grace Byer

WORDS ARE POWERFUL

Adjective Changers' Pledge:

I pledge to leave all my friends and family filled with wonderful adjectives that I will be proud of for generations to come!

THE MIRROR CHALLENGE

At the end of the day, think about all the adjectives you have shared throughout the day both good and bad, and say them to yourself while looking in the mirror. Think about how you feel as you say them and then imagine how you made the people that received your adjectives feel today. Did you leave everyone you encounter with positive adjectives?

ADJECTIVE KEEPERS

The following pages contain Adjective Keepers that I asked over 90 children, ages seven to ten years old, to fill in after explaining inside and outside adjectives. The adjectives that you see on the outside are the ones they find not true about themselves. The ones on the inside are the ones they own and believe to be true. You can find a version of this to do with your children in the *Awesome Adjective Changers* book. Any identifying features have been removed in an attempt to keep the anonymity of the children intact.

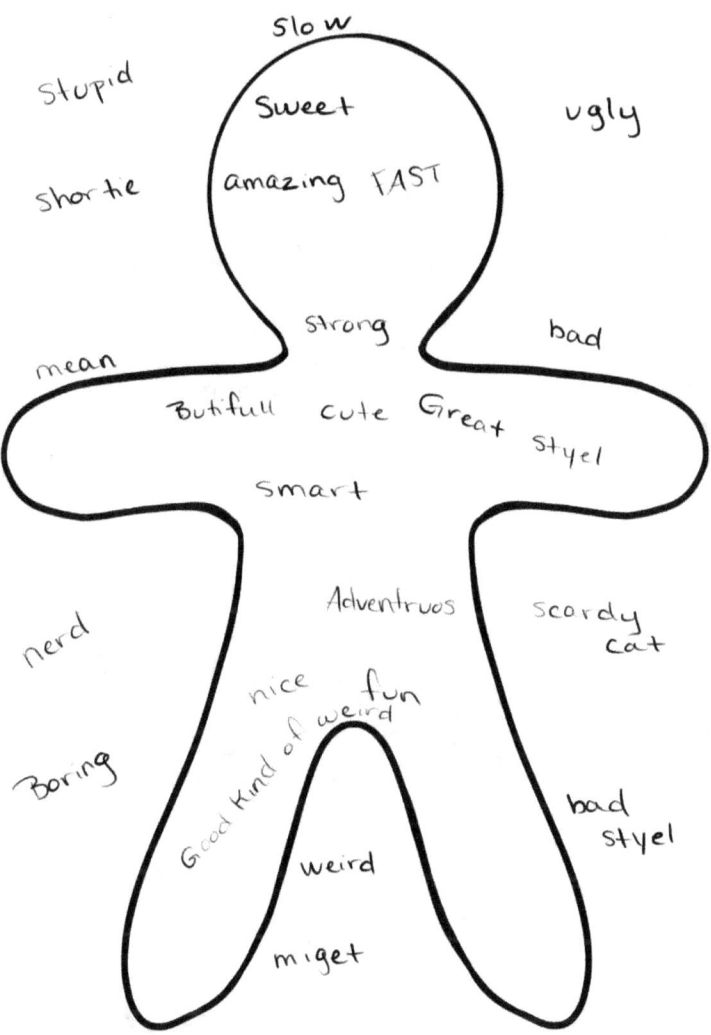

Head: Lonely Stupid Dumb unhappy violent annoying wierd insane bad bully Suicidall

Torso: happy good smart Loving great sane tense playful funny helpful

friendly memer

Left leg: sad sucks sad nerd hateful accidental creepy

Right leg: intense sucks nerd

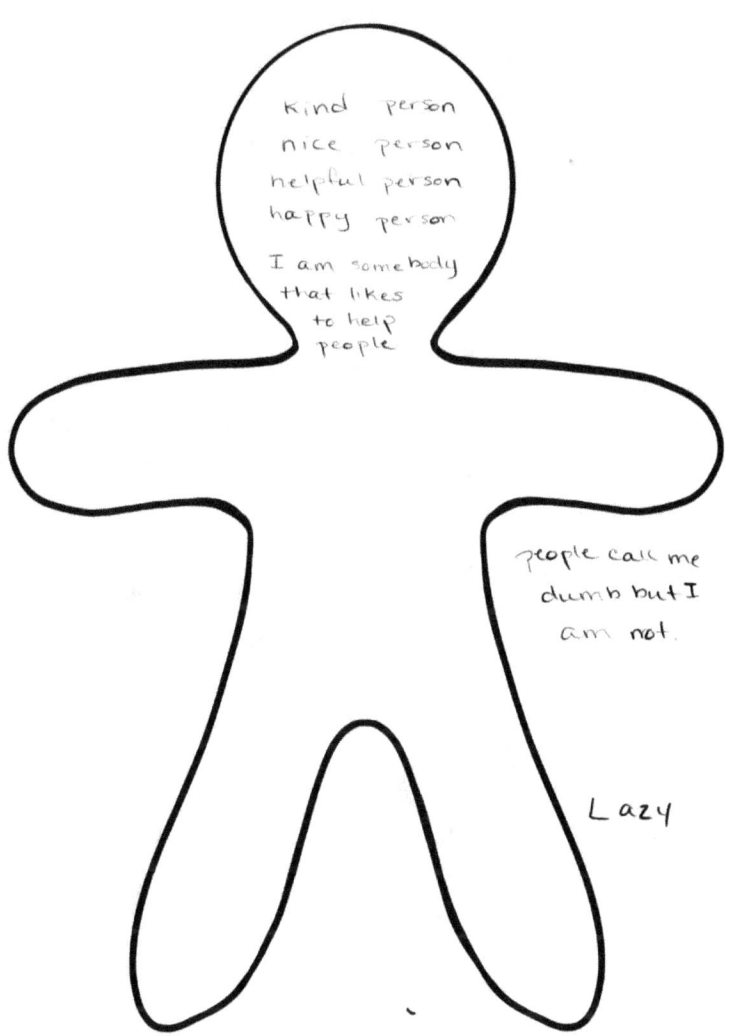

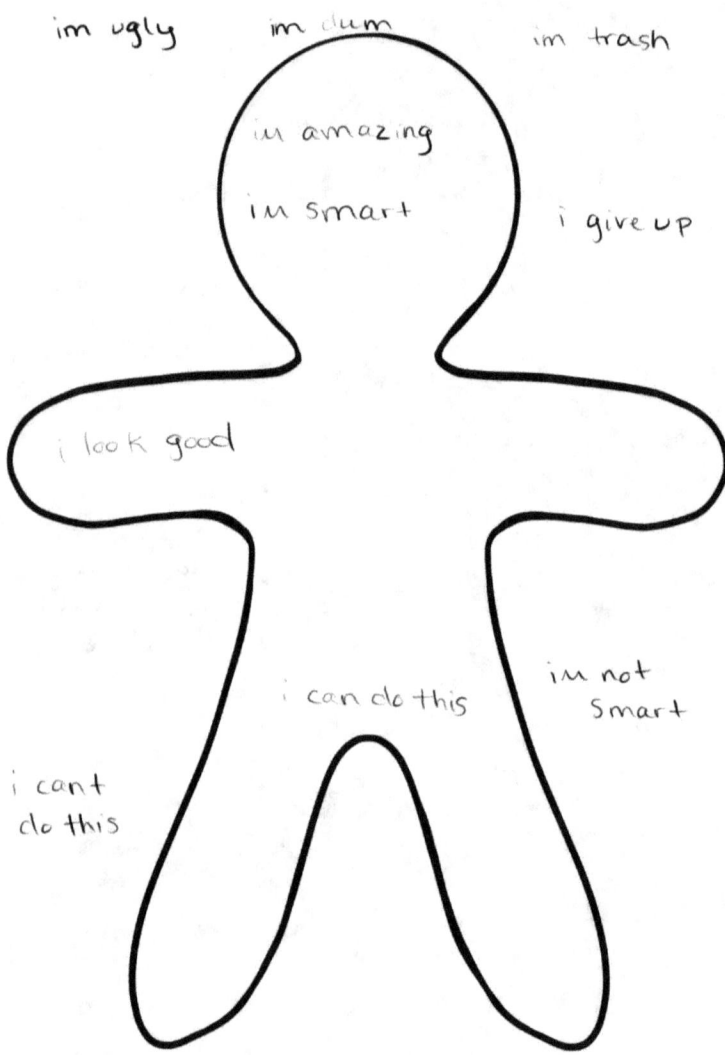

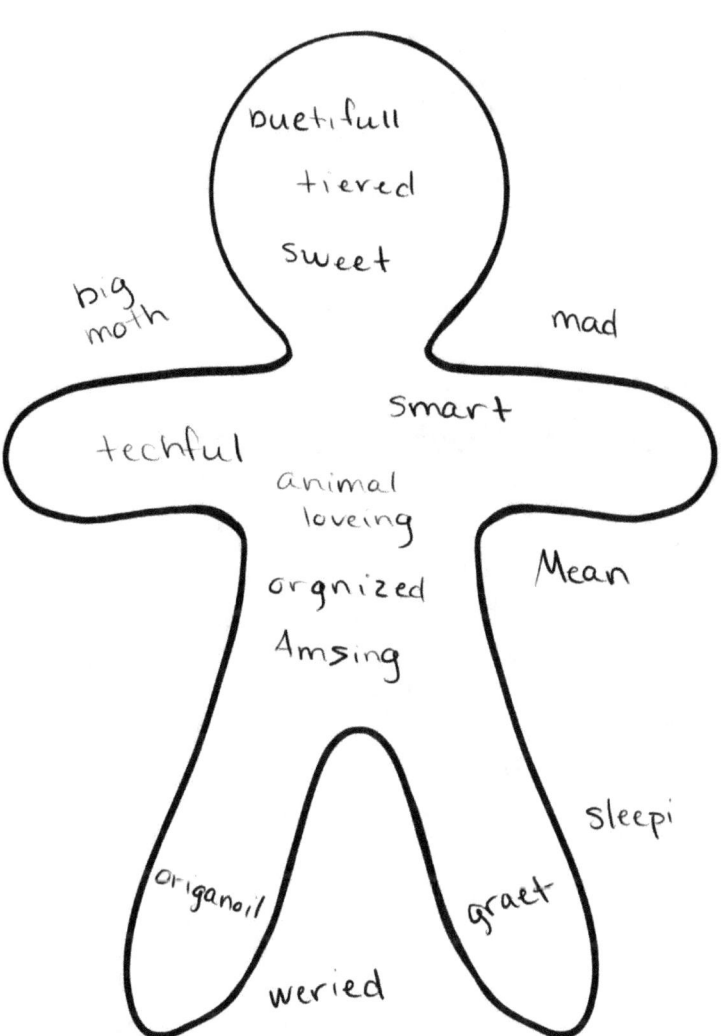

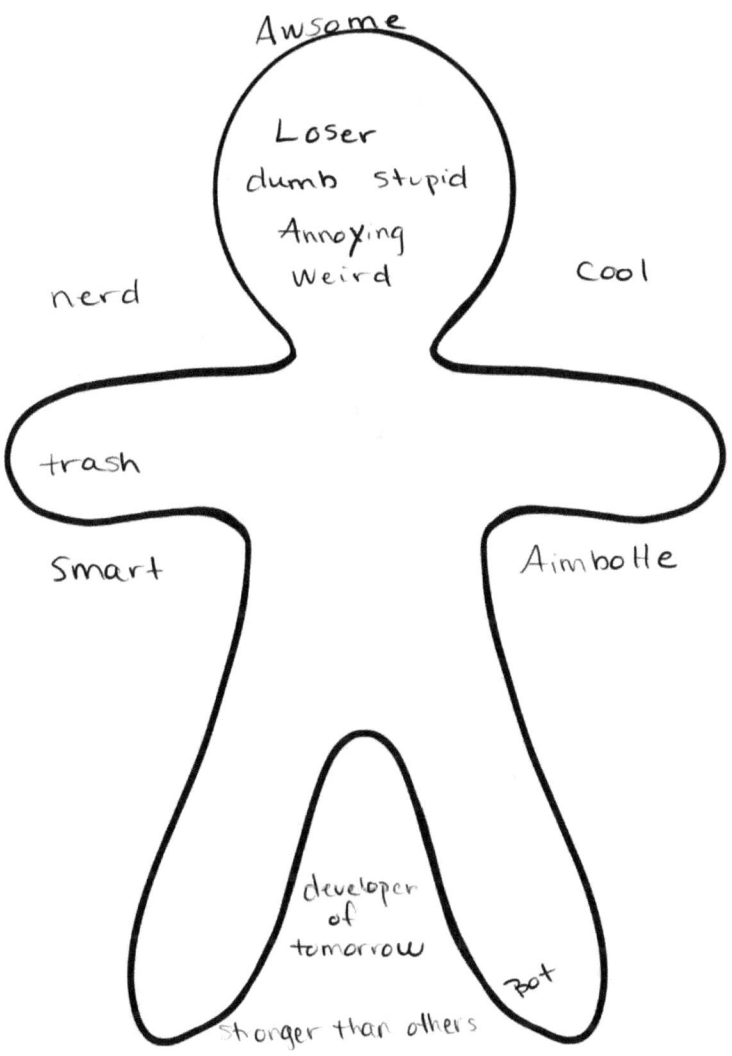

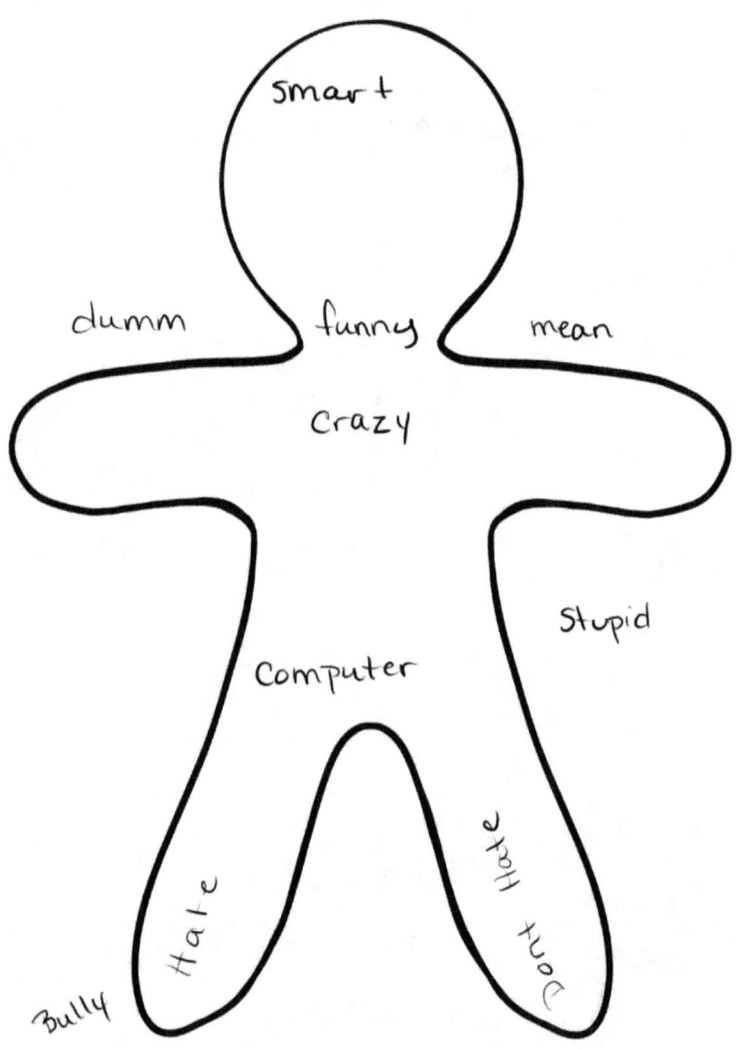

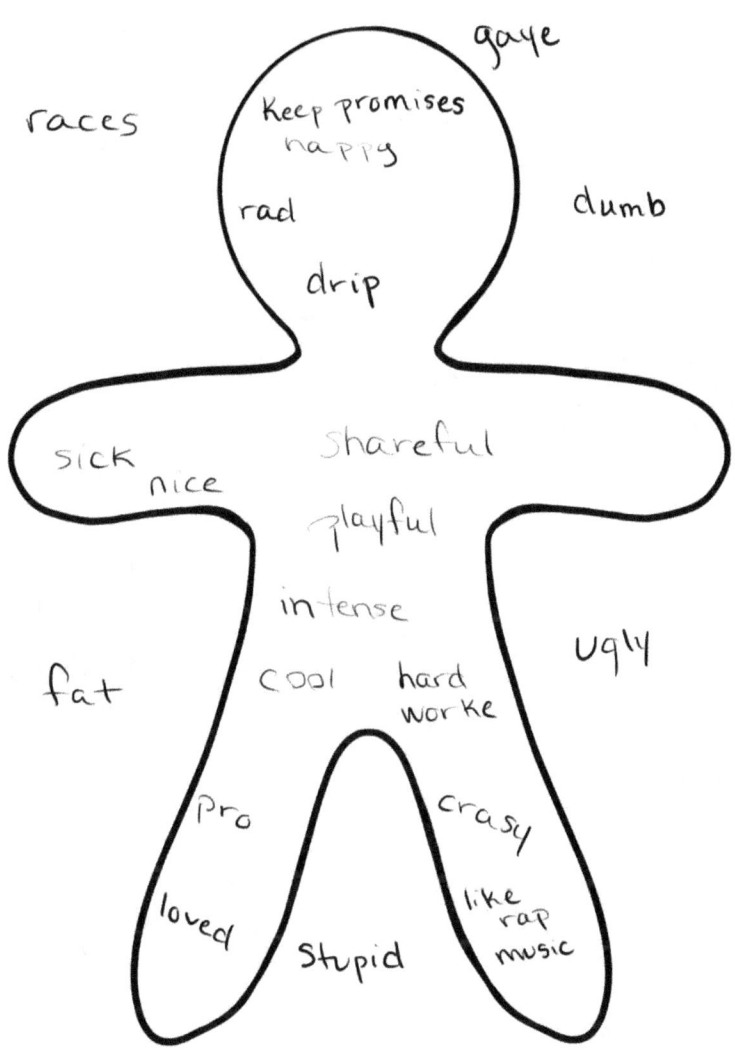

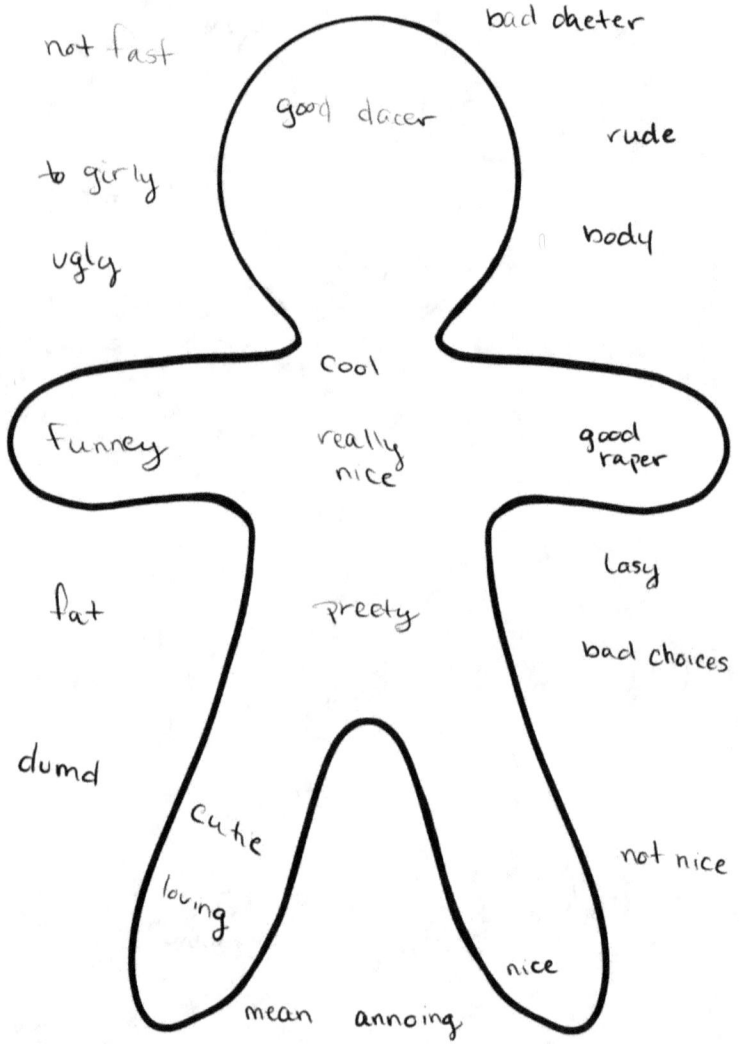

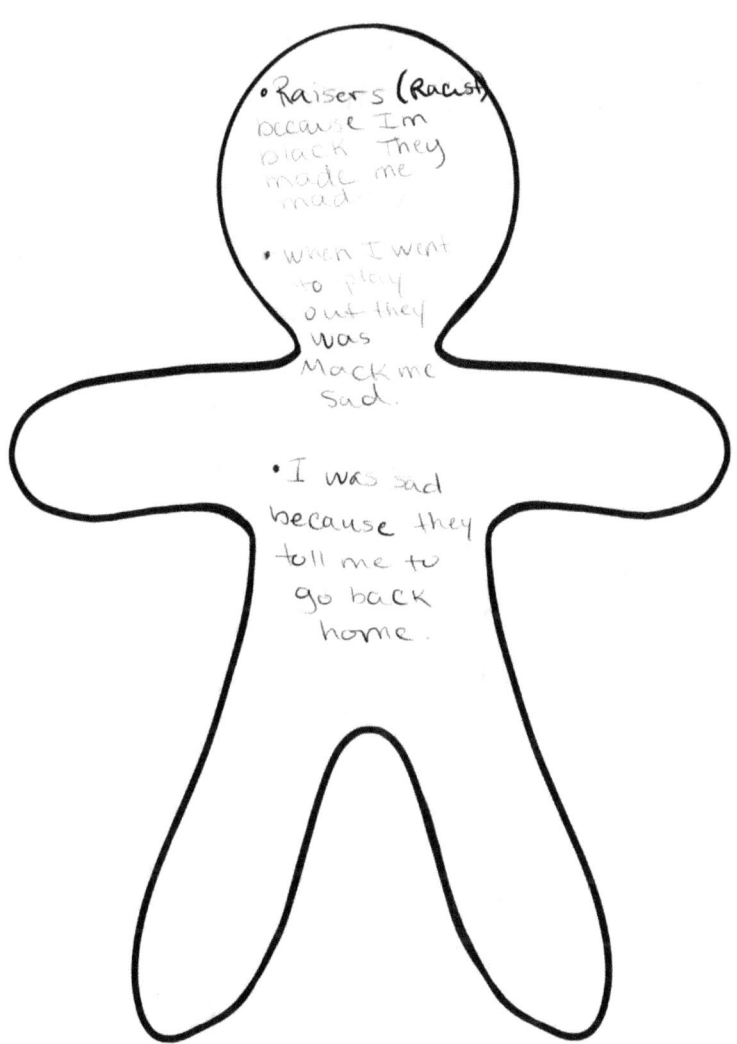

- Raisers (Racist) because I'm black. They made me mad.
- When I went to play out they was mack me sad.
- I was sad because they toll me to go back home.

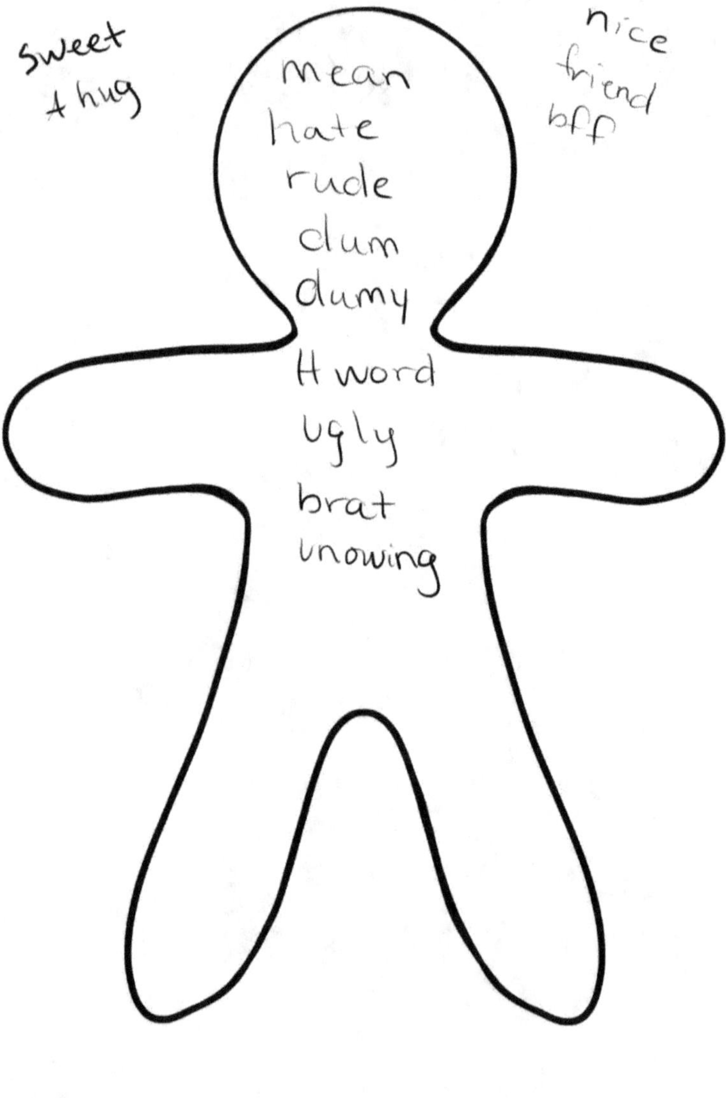

sweet
+ hug

nice
friend
bff

mean
hate
rude
dum
dumy
H word
ugly
brat
unowing

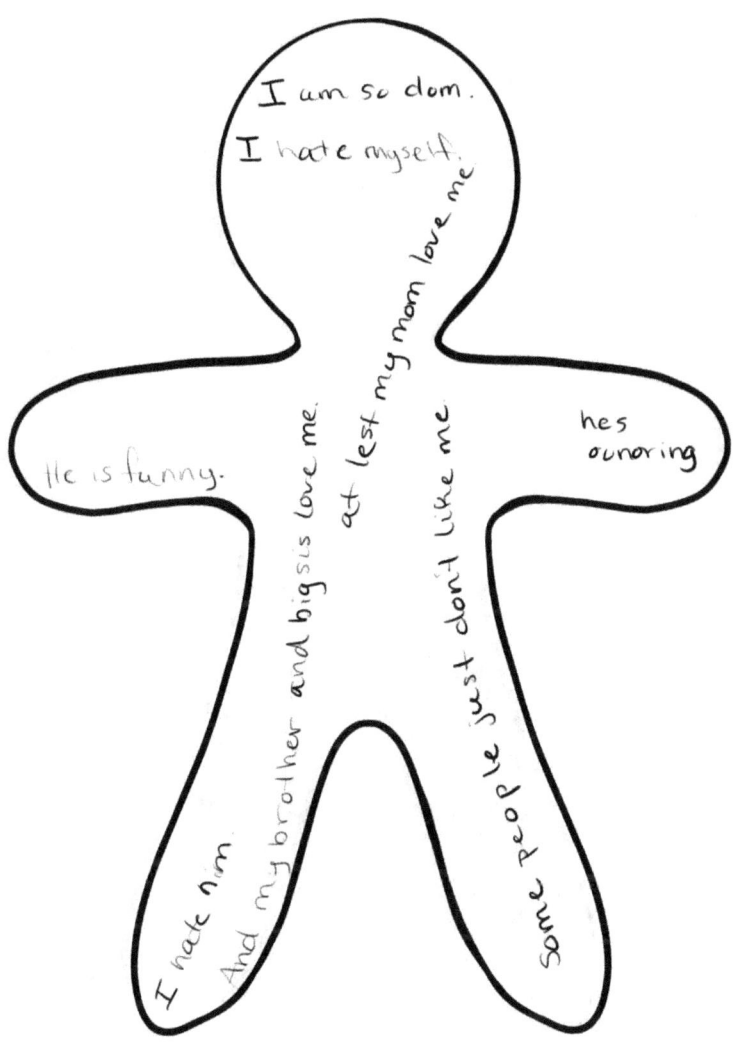

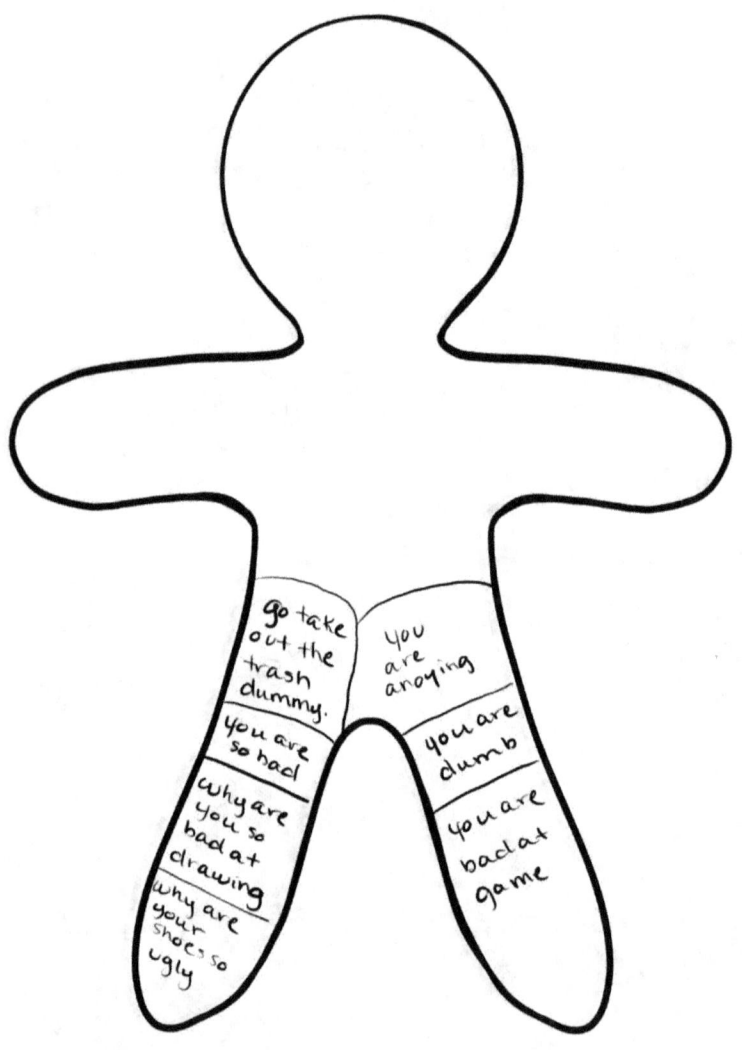

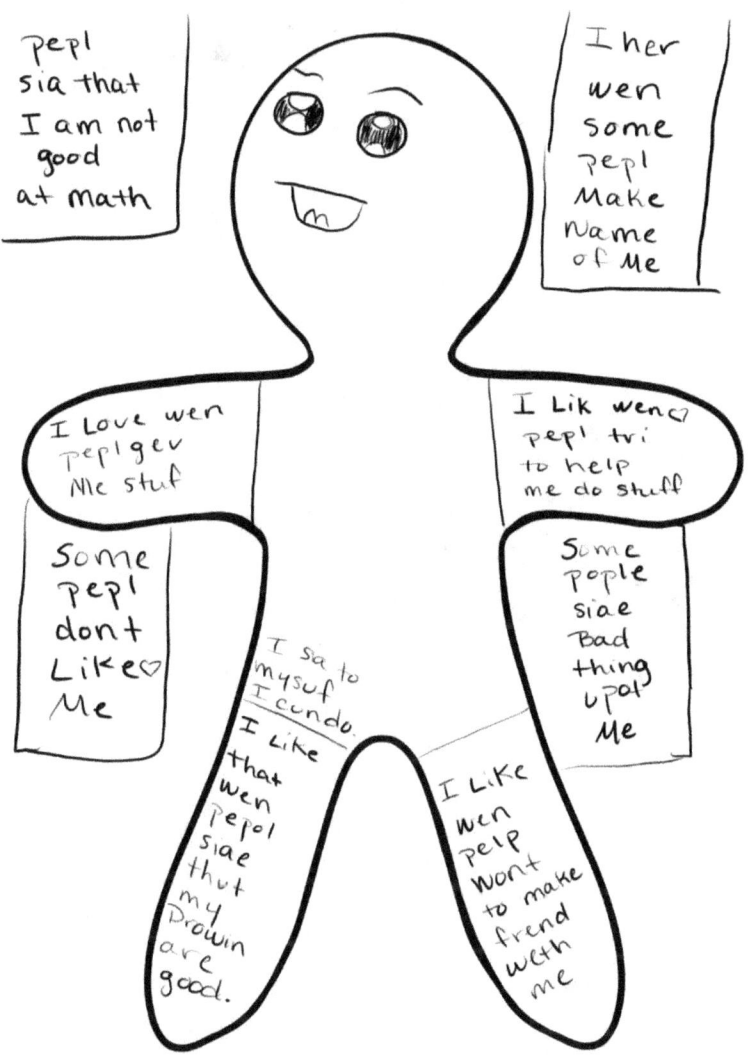

im beautifull.

I Love god.

People said they wanted to kill me. People said they wanted me to get run over by a car and some people just hated me. Girls wanted to jump me. a girl swung me and made me fall in kindergarden. and I wanted to kill myself.

I don't care what people say about me.

I Love my dogs and my family.

I think I'm cool and noone can stop me.

I don't let people mess with me cause they are jealous.

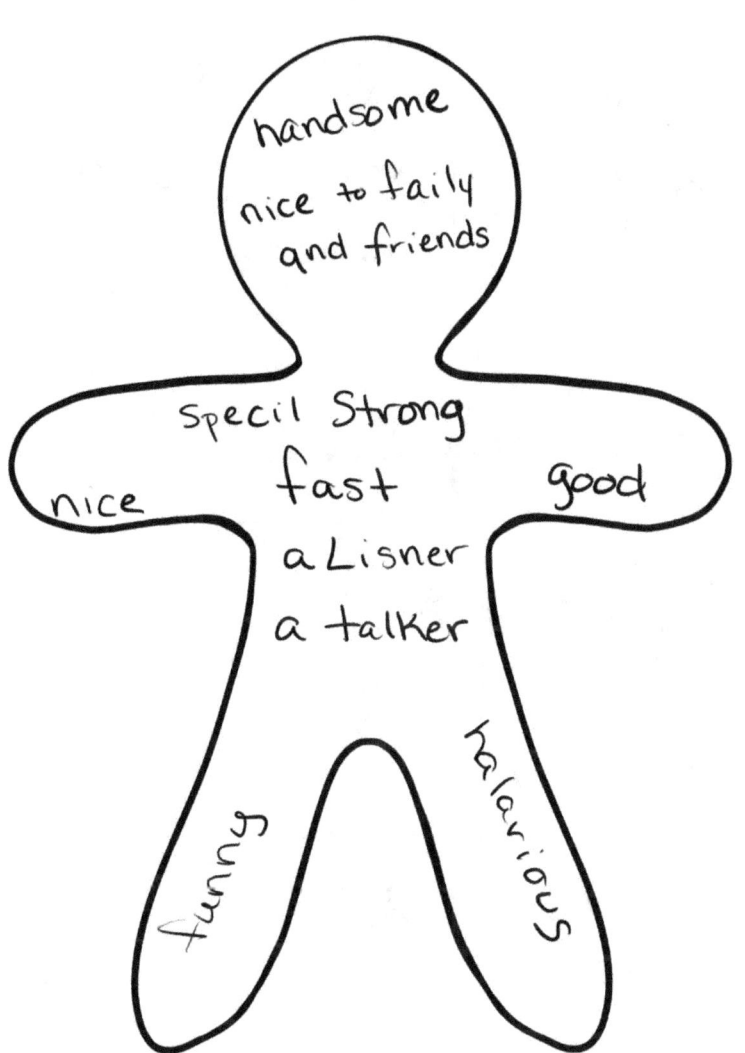

Head: people not being mean. people not calling me name.

Left of head: People being mean.

Right of head: People laughing at me if I get hurt.

Arms: People not laughing at me when I get hurt.

Torso: People who do not make fun of me. People not hurting me.

Left of body: people hurting me.

Right of body: being called names.

Leg: made fun of.

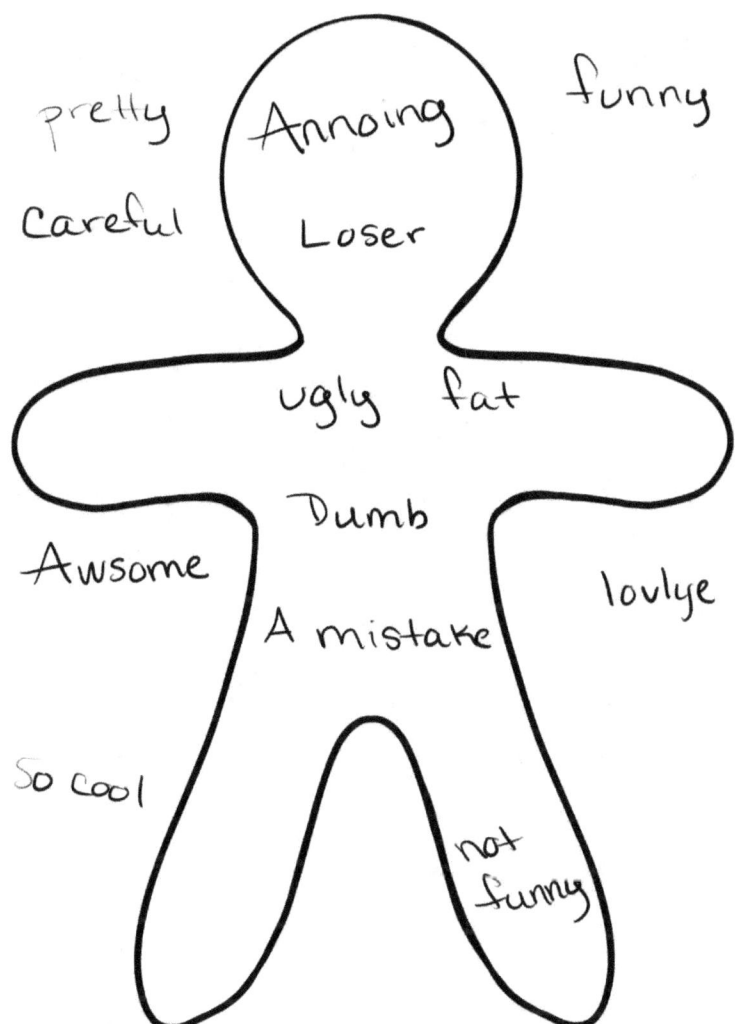

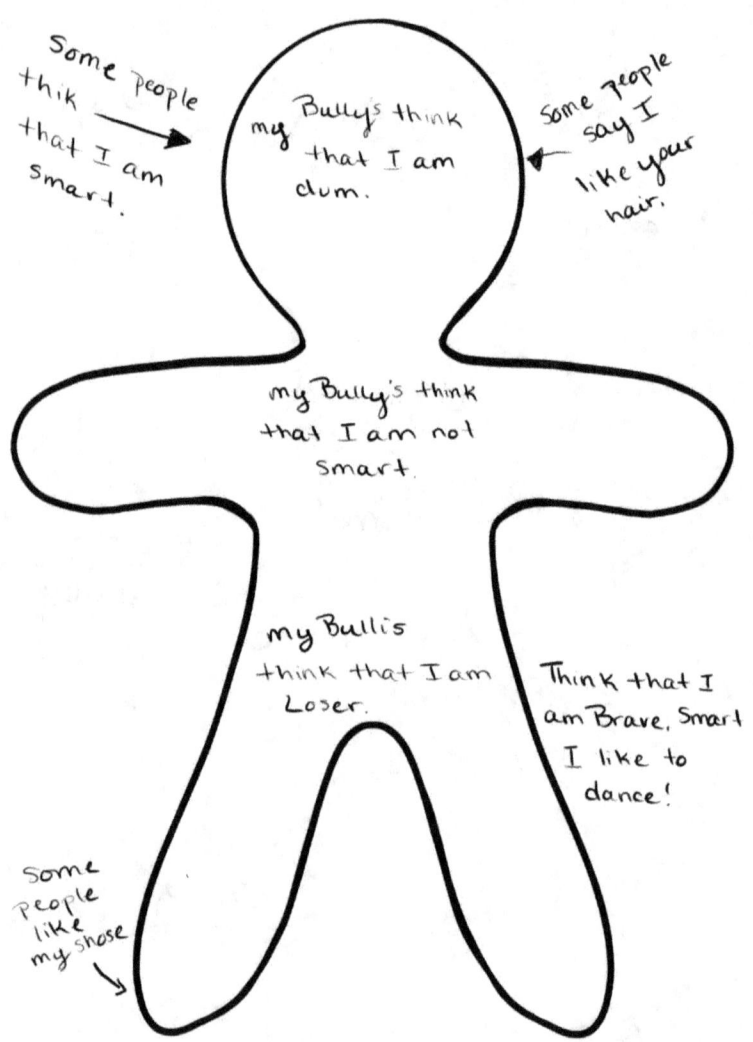

ABOUT THE AUTHOR

JANICE RIALS holds a master's degree in education, is a thirty-six-year veteran of pre-school to sixth grade retired educator, and was awarded the distinct honor of the 2018–2019 Local School Teacher of The Year. She is the author of three outstanding books, *There is No Moon at My House: Parenting Advice from a Veteran School Teacher*, *Awesome Adjective Changers*, and *Changing America's Adjectives One Child at a Time*. She lives in Georgia near her brother, daughter, three grandchildren, and her two grand-dogs Buttercup and Toby. She loves hosting family gatherings, walking trails, and spending time with her family.

www.ingramcontent.com/pod-product-compliance
Lightning Source LLC
Chambersburg PA
CBHW070334120526
44590CB00017B/2879